AF521942

CHIEF "TYEE" JOHN

VALLEY OF THE ROGUES

By PERCY T. BOOTH

Special Acknowledgement

The author wishes to thank Elwin Frye, retired, of Cave Junction, Oregon, for his valuable assistance in preparing this account of the early customs and living conditions of the Rogue River Indians.

Very little information about this vanished tribe has been printed, or is available. Many of the facts here related, are possible only because of his remarkable recall, aided by records and notes handed down and carefully preserved, containing information about the Rogues extending back in time, more than a hundred years.

Percy T. Booth

ISBN: 1-885813-00-7
Library of Congress Catalogue Card - 73-148275

First printing June 1971
Second printing December 1972
Third printing November 1993
Fourth printing April 2003

B&B PUBLISHING
63418 Everett Road
Coos Bay, OR 97420

My father, Percy T. Booth was himself a true pioneer of the Rogue Valley. Born on what was known as the "Heath" ranch in North Grants Pass in November of 1909, he left his beloved Rogue Valley only for short stints to find work during the depression, and again during World War II. There, he and his wife Ruth served as radio operators at a CAA (now FAA) weather station in Unalakleet, Alaska. That carefully written diary, he photographed, and left to me unpublished through Mom Ruth, was a precious legacy.

It is now published as *Alaska Diary.*

Percy Thomas Booth, was a remarkable writer, whose feelings and descriptions of the Rogue Valley and its early inhabitants came not from his pen, but from his heart. To his memory, I dedicate the fourth printing of *Valley of the Rogues.*

Richard A. Booth

Introduction

When the early explorers, trappers and traders cautiously edged their way westward into the wild, new Oregon Country, they found Indians as varied in manner and characteristics, as the country itself.

Although they found no tribes, great in numbers, having many thousands of warriors as did the Iroquois or Sioux, several of the Oregon tribes left indelible impressions, despite their lack in quantity.

In the Northwest, dwelt the Chinooks, a unique tribe whose remarkable developments in economic, social and ritual practices were unchallenged, from east to west.

Few examples match the great sacrifices made by the stubborn Nez Perce, skillfully led by Chief Joseph, in their gallant struggle for freedom against the invading white man.

And, in Oregon's last frontier, secure in the tight little valleys of the Rogue Country, lived the Rogues - by name and by nature.

This is their story, and how they lived - in their beloved Rogueland - before the coming of the white man.

Chapter One

The Oregon Country before 1840 was a vast area of unsettled wilderness, mostly unexplored, except for a few of the main valleys and waterways. Its boundary lines were indefinite. In general, it included the present states west of the Rocky Mountains and north of Spanish held California. Other than nomadic traders and trappers stripping what they could from the raw frontier, there was little interest in the land or its development.

Beginning in the early 1840s, the first attempts at settlement began when a trickle of hardy immigrants, mostly missionaries and their followers, challenged the wilderness, building a place for themselves in this wild new country.

It was the beginning of the end of British domination in the Northwest. Spain was soon to relinquish her claims to all land south of a line that eventually was to become the Oregon-California border. Slowly, the Americans pushed south of the Columbia River, into the rich and fertile Willamette Valley, in their search for farming land.

It was nearly ten years after that, before settlers ventured into the rugged regions of Southern Oregon, to take up land for homes and farming. The Rogue and Umpqua valleys had been merely travel routes to California and were always considered hostile and dangerous.

The journals of the Lewis and Clark expedition of 1805, contain some of the earliest known information about Oregon Indian tribes. Their studies and records were an important step in bringing about the early development of the far west. Together, with other extensive amounts of valuable information about the territory in general, theirs were the first official attempts at gathering statistics about the Oregon natives. However, it was later learned that the information, was in some cases, inaccurate. Apparently, much of the data was taken directly from the natives through interpreters. Their scant knowledge of the country, other than the immediate area in which they lived, and their meager understanding of distance and time led to errors limiting its value.

The degree of success the early traders in the Oregon Country could enjoy, depended to a great extent on their ability to build friendly relations with the natives.

Some of the earliest of contacts with western Indians were with tribes living along the Columbia River. Of all the far west tribes, the trappers and traders particularly cultivated the friendship of the peaceful Chinooks, to their trading advantage.

Over the years, British, French and American traders developed a curious language, that was to become known as Chinook jargon. Actually, it was a mixture of Indian, English and French. It was gradually adopted by most of the tribes, as well as the early pioneers, as a universal means of communications. Its use spread from California to Alaska.

Living along the north side of the Columbia, in the vicinity of the river that now bears their name, dwelt the Klickitats. They had a talent for trading, surpassing all others. Their location made it favorable for them to act as intermediaries between the tribes along the coast and those of the interior. They were quite active and enterprising in their dealings with white traders, who gave them the nickname, "The Indian Jews of the Oregon Country".

It is possible that much of their ability as traders stemmed from the results of a great epidemic occuring in the 1820s, that raged through the tribes of the Willamette Valley. The Klickitats, uneffected by the disease, quickly took advantage of the weakened condition of the valley tribes, invading their territory and ranging as far south as the edges of southern Oregon and the holdings of the Umpquas. Eventually, they were driven back to their own territory, but in their conquests they gained valuable information about the country, its tribes, their languages and customs. The early Oregon explorers and military men often sought out the Klickitats as guides and interpreters.

Indians living along the coast and in the areas immediately dominated by the Pacific ocean's climate and its marine influence, held a marked physical and mental difference from those of the interior.

The immense area of the great Pacific exerted a preponderant effect on the Indian inhabitants, greatly influencing the patterns of their existence. The abundance of rain and rich soil supported a wild and vigorous growth of tangled vegetation. The numerous streams provided excellent waterways for canoe travel, thus avoiding the difficulties encountered by dense brush and timber growth. As the rivers neared the ocean they flattened out, ran more slowly and emptied into bays and inlets. There, lived an abundant and unending supply of fresh and salt water fish and other marine life, which was easy to take with a minimum of effort and equipment.

The ocean's temperature remaining almost constant winter and summer, warmed the cooler inland air in the winter, as it flowed against the coastal regions, making snow and freezing conditions unusual. The same conditions held summer temperatures to a moderate degree. The mild climate and favorable conditions, the abundance of easy to procure food - mainly, rich, oily fish - produced a race of natives shaped by their local environment. Physically, the coast dwellers were short and thick-bodied, of mediocre physique, with little initiative and not particularly alert in mind and action. Their friendly surroundings and their abundant food supply offered them little challenge of imagination, or need of being vigorous or aggressive.

Local conditions did much to dictate the physical characteristics of the interior natives in the same manner as the coastal tribes, but with entirely different results. With tall ranges of coastal mountains brushing back two-thirds of the rainfall before it passed their crests, the interior valleys and higher plateaus did not support the rank growth of vegetation found along the ocean belt. The wild and fast flowing streams were not ideally suited to canoe travel, as were the coastal rivers. Thus, a country more open in nature, timbered, but not as brushy, and having more prominant grazing areas, supported a different type of wild game and promoted more travel by horse and foot.

Nature had stocked those jeweled inland hills and valleys throughout the Rogue Country, with teeming hoards of every imaginable game animal. Great herds of deer, elk, goats, antelope, mountain sheep and bear, as well as huge numbers of small animals, ranged unhindered throughout the area. In fact, wild game, fish and natural foods were so plentiful before the coming of the white man, that the Rogue River Indians were one of only two tribes in the entire United States, that cultivated no food crops of any kind, depending completely on nature's supplies for their existence.

There is reason to believe the Indians did grow some tobacco, but it is thought that such cultivation was only after the plants had been introduced by the whites, or possibly obtained by trading with California tribes, where it had been introduced earlier by the Spanish.

Even though there was a great abundance of game, it required a continuous activity of aggressive strength and cunning alertness by the Rogues, to keep themselves supplied with food and the necessary materials for clothing and shelter. Unlike their coastal cousins food could not always be obtained with the ease of throwing a salmon spear or dipping a net. There was no such thing as a lazy Rogue.

Scattered throughout the boundaries of Oregon as we know them today, were nearly fifty major tribes of Indians. Many of them were not great in numbers, those in southwestern Oregon often being small bands of less than fifty, ranging up to tribes of several hundred. It has been variously estimated that the entire Rogue tribe including women and children, numbered less than six hundred.

The dominate feature of remote and rugged southwestern Oregon was the clear, cold waters of a beautiful stream rising high in the perpetual snow banks and underground springs of the white-capped Cascades. That wild and untamed river set its course westward and without a backward glance raced its way through a hundred and fifty miles of sheer rock chasms, Eden-like valleys, and tree-green canyons, until finally out of breath, it settled in rest in the broad lap of the Pacific.

It was the general practice of early-day frontiersmen to name the Indian tribes after some specific geographical area in which they lived, or perhaps, to name the area after the inhabitants. It is commonly agreed that the river draining the southern section of Oregon was named after the tribe of Indians living along its midcourse.

Trappers and traders in the early 1840s, were referring to the river as the "Rogue's River", the name arising from the character of the local Indians. French trappers exploring southward, were some of the first to spread accounts of the troubles and treachery encountered with the natives, calling them, "Les Coquins", or The Rascals. The stream, they called, "La Riviere aux Coquins", The River of the Rogues.

Another accounting states the French found the river flowing bank-full of red, mud-stained water from the wash of its tributaries, and called the stream, "The Rogue", or, The Red. However, the first explanation is the one most commonly accepted.

In 1854, the Oregon Territorial legislature believing the river should have an official and legal name changed it to Gold River, and it is shown as such on early maps. But the new name met with little favor among the early residents of the Rogue Valley and was soon dropped and forgotten.

If the name is picturesque, it was also well chosen. There is hardly a word in the dictionary that could better describe the area, the river, and its people. It matters little whether the locality received its name from the character of the Indians, or the inhabitants were named after the river, for in either case it is suitable and warranted.

"The primeval Rogue River—
A favorite Indian fishing spot where the big ones leaped the falls."

"Tranquil environment and mildness of climate made a near paradise in Rogue River country."

Chapter Two

The Rogues, in general, occupied the Rogue and Illinois watersheds from the mouth of the Illinois River, south and east to the Siskiyou mountain range. They were also scattered along the northern bank of the Rogue and its tributaries and the upper drainages of Cow Creek. Farther up-river, they claimed the Bear Creek Valley, the upper Applegate and Jacksonville country, and the expanse of valleys and foothills surrounding the Table Rock area.

Although the common and popular name applied to these natives of the Rogue Valley and its surrounding areas was "The Rogues" this distinctive and unique tribe was officially called "The Takelmas". In the division of tribes in southern Oregon, ethnologists applied the name "Takelma", while that of Rogues, was earned by reputation, at least in the opinion of the valley's early-day settlers.

Spilling over the Siskiyou mountains from northern California, elements of the Shasta tribe occupied in harmony with the Takelmas the hunting grounds above the mouth of Stuart Creek - now known as Bear Creek - as well as portions of Little Butte Creek and its headwaters, to the base of Snowy Butte, now called Mount McLoughlin.

This restricted group has been determined a separate, although closely allied tribe, from those residing in the lower valleys and the mid-Rogue section. The name, "Latgwa", meaning in the Takelma language, "those living in the uplands", has been applied to this subdivided group.

Although there was strong Shasta influence, they were culturally identical with the Takelmas and spoke the same language. The two groups frequently intermarried. Early studies of these tribes name only one village as being Latgwa. It was located in the vicinity of the present town of Jacksonville.

The native name for the general Rogue tribe was "da-gel-ma", meaning; "Those dwelling along the river". It is not clear how the name Takelma was applied. It is quite likely a corruption of the word, "da-gel-ma".

One explanation of the origin of the tribe's name has been offered by Colonel T. M. Draper, who was engaged in early Waldo mining interests, and who, it is said, was responsible for naming a small settlement on the east fork of the Illinois River "Taklamah" after a local Indian chief. It is possible that such a minor chief existed in that area, but neither his name or any reference to him seems to appear in any early historical writings.

All of the historians of early Oregon agree that the Rogue Indians were considered to be one of, if not the most intelligent, cunning and war-like tribes in the Territory. They were a completely uncivilized and barbarous people, practically untouched by the influence of white traders working along the coast, and in the Columbia River regions. Little, if any, early Spanish influence in California found its way north, to the interior of southwestern Oregon.

Although there is little definite information available, indicating exactly where the Rogues came from, or how long they had lived in these regions, it seems likely they were a part of the immigration across the ancient land bridge from Siberia. The fact that they had no written language severely held back any record of their history, and the natural result of written records - the beginnings of civilization.

The men were large of frame, upright in bearing, generally of open countenance and intelligent of expression. Their faces were broad and oval shaped, with medium, high cheek bones, a wide mouth, thin lips and a flat chin. Their eyes had a squinting, half-closed characteristic, giving them a look of determined purpose; a look which a great many whites interpreted as proof of their treachery and meanness. They were proud, brave and fearless warriors.

The women were generally lighter in skin tone, neater in their personal habits, and more graceful in their carriage and movements, than those of other Oregon tribes.

Army officers who met the Rogue warriors in combat were continually amazed at their ability to perform maneuvers unexpected of uncivilized savages. They were one of the few tribes in the west making use of dirt and log fortifications in their engagements with their white enemies.

There is little to be found in today's Rogue River Valley, that indicates the exceptional nature of its early Indian inhabitants. Very few geographical locations have inherited Indian names to keep the birthright of its former sons and daughters alive.

The present-day residents of southern Oregon see little to indicate the area is rich with a bold, blazing history of bloody Indian battles, and a fantastic gold rush, that led frenzied miners to uncover millions of dollars of the "yellow plague of greed". It equaled on a smaller scale, California's days of '49 and the Klondike of 1887.

Much has been lost of the primitive history, culture and arts, of the Rogue River Indians. Other than a series of official government reports dealing with their language, and a limited account of their life and customs, little is known of this long-ago vanished tribe. The meager history of their way of life that has been preserved, is for the most part, only an incidental portion of the recordings of their long and bitter struggle with the white man.

After their last great battles, their numbers drastically reduced by policies of extermination, they were banned from their native homeland and placed on reservations in localities strange and unsuited to their former way of life. As has so often been the case, they quickly fell prey to many of the diseases of the white man. What was left of their tribe was further terribly decimated by epidemics, and by 1911 a government count showed that only six of the once proud and haughty Rogue warriors remained.

Ethnologists have found it difficult to divide and identify Indian tribes by definite areas and boundaries. Although the various tribes, did in general, claim and control certain domains, their movements were often fluid and indefinite. A tribe might occupy an area for many years, then be forced from their hunting grounds by an invading tribe. The disposed ones, in order to exist, would then search for territory they could successfully conquer. And so the chain of events would continue. To a lesser degree, the same conditions were sometimes brought about by a scarcity of game or by epidemics. In the far west the tribal separations became even more confusing. They were so sharply defined in some localities, that a tribe might be limited to even one small village.

The natives of southwestern Oregon were not greatly influenced by any organized governmental tribal structure, other than their immediate local groups. Even the smallest of bands had their own sub-chiefs, who were sub-chiefs only in the sense their bands were smaller in numbers than others, of the same language and customs. As sub-chiefs, they were not strictly bound to other larger chieftianships.

Because it has been difficult to define tribal areas except for definite time periods, it has become common practice to use the language, or dialect, as an identifying means.

Due to many natural divisions of the land areas of southern Oregon by high, rugged mountain ranges, and the difficulties of travel, many tribes, sub-tribes, and lesser bands, were found living in their own secluded and isolated valleys. In some cases they would speak dialects quite different from their nearest neighbors. The more lofty the mountain ranges the longer the snow cover would remain, making travel difficult for several months of the year, thereby holding the tribes in greater isolation. This fact, together with the general advantage of a great amount of game, limited the need for ranging afar for food, encouraging a wider difference in language variations to develop. Twelve different linguistic families were found in Oregon at the time of the coming of the white man.

Several things about the Rogue Indians single them out as unique and outstanding among the tribes of southwestern Oregon. The most remarkable of these, was the fact that they spoke a different language than those tribes surrounding their native holdings. Historians and those who specialize in the study of native languages offer no explanation for this puzzling circumstance.

Most of the neighboring tribes in southern Oregon spoke a language belonging to a linguistic group known as, "Athapascan". The great Athapascan linguistic stock was found scattered over a wide area of the west. Tribes using that language were living in parts of Oklahoma, Colorado, New Mexico, Wyoming and Arizona. At least one tribe in Washington belonged to the Athapascan group, and eight or more in southern Oregon. This same basic language family found its way northward to Canada and even as far as Alaska.

The Athapascan linguistic stock is often linked with the Apache Indians, probably because they were great in number, with their many associated tribes, and so well known over the southwest for their many years of fierce and stubborn resistance to the white man.

The language spoken by the Rogues was not merely a different dialect than that of other tribes in southern Oregon. Edward Sapir, government ethnologist, who carried out the leading research on the Takelma language in 1909, said; "With the Athapascan dialects of southwestern Oregon . . . practically no agreements of detail are traceable. Takelma stands entirely isolated among its neighbors."

Most Indian tongues are considered difficult to speak and Takelma was a definite example of that opinion. By comparison with other Indian dialects it was even more harsh in tone and lacking in musical inflection.

Stress and pitch were important. Many words that were identical were identified only by the pitch applied to the pronounciation, especially if it was the last syllable of a sentence. It was common for Takelma to seek a rise in pitch at sentence endings, rather than a fall.

To compound the unfamiliar difficulties was the method of using entirely different words to cover a class of objects with a single meaning. For example; we use the word heart, interchangeably, whether we refer to a man, a bird, or a fish. In Takelma, a separate word was used in each case, identifying the class in which it was used. It is not difficult to understand why the early pioneers developed the Chinook jargon, for its use, together with sign language, made it possible to communicate with different tribes even though they spoke different dialects.

Counting was accomplished by using both words and hand signs. Numbers up to five, were spoken as words, while six was indicated by one finger laid across the palm of the out-stretched hand. Two fingers was seven, and three, eight - but nine was signified by placing two fingers twice, that is, five, plus two, plus two. The teens were expressed by both hands (ten fingers) held up, then one finger above, and so on. Twenty, was one man, that is, both hands and both feet.

Even though a person may have had a speaking knowledge of Takelma a great deal of difficulty still existed, due to the fact there were many cases in which no Takelma word existed to use interchangeably with English.

The Takelmas enjoyed story telling and their legends were handed down through generations of father to son, and family to family. As with all primitive people they attempted to explain the mysteries of life, by applying their stories and myths to creatures with which they were familiar.

One of those stories, a charming myth, as told by an aged Takelma woman has been preserved. It is a good example of the difficulties encountered in translating from Takelma to English.

Some explanation is necessary about the characters in the story. The coyote was always a favorite character in Indian mythology, and with the Takelmas this was no exception. The wily coyote was much admired and respected for his cunning stealth, and his ability to outmaneuver his stronger and better armed adversaries. It was considered an honor to be compared to his shrewd instinct and great endurance.

The second character in the myth is a large black long-legged beetle, called "Roasting-Dead-People". No doubt there was a reason for such a bizarre name, but none was given. Apparently, the awkward and slow-moving insect seemed a good symbol to represent death. The rambling myth, with some difficulty, attempts to explain the mysteries of death and the reason dead people don't return to life. Here is presented an English version, translated from Takelma:

> "Roasting-Dead-People, his child it died. He and Coyote, neighboring each other, they were. And then, that he said to him; "Blanket, lend it to me", he said, it is said, Roasting-Dead-People. "Not blanket, I lend to you, for where will there be dead people, if they return?" He said, it is said, Coyote. And then next door he returned, Roasting-Dead-People.

He buried it, his child, who had died. And then it is said, long time it became. Now, it is said, Coyote, his child, sick it became. Now it died. Now next door he went. "Blanket lend it to me, my child since it died." "What you said?" Roasting-Dead-People, that he said. "Last time when I said, blanket lend it to me, you said, "People, where will they be if they return?" So Coyote returned and buried his child. "And for that reason, people do not nowadays return when they die."

A second story, told by the same Takelma woman, is not only an interesting example of the language, but a detailed explanation of building a Takelma house.

"People, house they make it. Post, they set down, and here again they set it down, yonder again they set it down, in four places they set them down. Then, also they place (beam) across. Then, and just there, house, its wall, they make it; then and on top thereof, they put them house boards, sugar pine those boards they make them. And then from on top they finish it, and from on top, hold (hole) they make it. Smoke there is going out. And then ladder they make it. They notch it in several places. Down to earth going, they make it. And then they finish it all cleaned in side. And then mats they spread them out, inside, of that kind, there on they sit, people. Fire, its place in center, so they being seated on both sides of fire. In that way, long ago, people, for the most part, build their house in winter. But in summer, this way they sit, not in house there in."

The last sentence of the story is explained by the fact that at the time of the telling, the story teller was seated outside in the open.

During the warm weather period of the year the Takelmas moved from place to place following the cycle of the season's food supply, preparing for the coming winter. Their various camps were temporary and little effort was spent in developing permanent shelter. Summer camps might be nothing more than a ring of brush thrown-up to encircle their campfire, or a skin or two on one side of an up-rooted tree, or the shelter of a friendly over-hanging rock ledge.

In the description of Takelma house building reference is made to the time as "long ago" when the old squaw was a young woman in her native village of Dak-ts-asin, on Jump-off-Joe Creek; but the use of boards indicate the time was after the white man had introduced his building methods.

Another interesting legend passed down through generations of father and son was recorded in 1918, by Jake Eern, an ancient and last survivor of the Umpqua tribe.

In the times, when his father's father and his father's father before him, had seen many snows come and go, there dwelt a peaceful tribe of people in the Great Valley, where the shining river flowed like a morning string of dewdrops, around the great flat mountain of stone.

And then, there came another tribe to the valley, where lived the peaceful people, and they saw many deer in the green prairies and much fish in the river. And there came about a war, between these people and for many suns, one after another, there was fighting.

And then one night, when the valley people laid down their robes to sleep, the invaders crept into their camp and with silent knives, killed the Chief's brother. And when the time was morning and the Chief saw his brother was dead, he looked on a mountain and saw many people against the rising sun and knew they were the evil ones that had done the deed. He held high, his war spear in one hand, and his war bow in the other, and cried out in terrible anguish, for the Great Spirit to turn the slayer to stone. And then, the Great Spirit did this thing, that was asked by the Chief of the peaceful people.

And, says Jake Eern, there is a big rock in Sam's Valley, covered with much moss, which is the body of the Big Chief. And the people took sharp stones and made marks on the rock, which told of these things and of other things, long before his father's time. Jake says that the rock, that is the Chief's body, is about five feet high and eight feet long, and that it is yet there, in the valley of the peaceful people, so that all who come to see will know, that his story speaks the truth.

There is still another interesting recollection of the long ago, when the Rogues, too, loved the little valley where Grants Pass now stands, and made it their home.

Mildred Butler Bryce, a lifetime resident of Josephine County, gave this writer two Indian arrowheads she found in 1903, when she was eight years old. The arrowheads are made from that favorite material, obsidian, black in color and somewhat translucent. Neither are perfect.

Mildred attended the first, second and third grades in an early-day school, located on the south side of Bridge street, just west of the point where Fourth street now intersects. The Oregon State Highway shops now stand on the old school site.

The school building was a one story shiplap structure, built in a "T" shape, with two rooms across the front and one room at the rear, center. Steps at the front and middle of the building led to a hall that split the two front rooms and extended to the single back room. The school was painted white, and for lack of a better name was called the "white school". At that time it was the only school south of the railroad tracks and was in use until the Riverside school was built in 1909. The teachers were Miss Aiken, first grade, Mollie Belding, second grade and Mrs. Hogan, third grade.

There were only a few houses west of the school and the uncleared land quickly became a tangle of manzanita brush, topped with a generous stand of pines.

Less than a half mile west of the school, and toward the river, there was an open spot in the timber about two hundred feet in diameter. There were several Indian grave-mounds in one portion of the clearing. Children from the "white school" often played there and sometimes scratched in the dirt looking for Indian relics. It was general knowledge at that time that the area was an old Indian camp. In those days, Indian graves were still reasonably common and were seldom disturbed. On several occasions arrowheads and beads were found, and the two arrow points mentioned were uncovered at that location.

The old Indian camp has long ago been covered by the white man's houses, and is now a thickly settled residential area. But there is little doubt, that at one time, the Rogues had their own little group of homes within what is now the city limits of Grants Pass.

Some of the earliest of explorers and traders along the Oregon Coast, particularly in the vicinity north of the Columbia River and along the Washington Coast, were amazed to find the Indians living in well constructed houses covered with pine or cedar boards.

Although it was possible for natives of that time and area, to split rough slabs from straight-grained logs with elk horn or stone tools, it is thought they entered the period of board construction after they had learned to fashion crude splitting tools from pieces of iron, found attached to timbers, washed up on the beach from shipwrecks.

These laboriously formed planks - a more suitable word than boards - had little in common with today's precision cut and satin-smooth lumber. The planks were about two inches thick, varying with the straightness of the grain of the log.

In order to make logs light enough to handle and short enough to split, they were burned into convenient lengths. A great variety of widths and lengths resulted. Whether or not the board was chipped and rubbed smooth, depended on its intended purpose.

If it was to be made into furniture, such as a bench, many hours - even days - might be spent rubbing its surface with polishing stones. Usually such stones were about four to eight inches across their flat surface. They were chipped and shaped to form a handle that would fit the palm of the hand. Different stones had different degrees of roughness - the Redman's sandpaper.

To the natives, the fashioning of each board represented days of labor and a wealth to cherish. Each one was carefully cared for and passed from generation to generation. Such boards were actually one of the commodities used in measuring personal wealth.

The implication that time was of value to an Indian may seem a little ridiculous, but actually, it was quite true. The continuing search by the Indians of the Rogue River Valley for food, for today and tomorrow never ended. If there was food to eat and plenty of skins for clothing, there were always arrowheads to chip, and shafts to scrape, and spears to repair. Nothing could be farther from the truth, that the wild and free life of a Rogue Indian was one of comfort and ease.

According to today's popular conception all Indians lived in cone-shaped teepees, made by lashing poles together and covering them with dappled animal skins, which were brightly decorated with wobbly swastikas and sinister eagles - their clutching talons serving as a warning to any proposed enemy.

It is true that such simple and portable shelters were used by many North American tribes, especially the plains Indians, who in their wanderings often found little in the way of materials with which to build shelter.

But that kind of symbolic teepee was not used by the Rogues. Their houses were usually built in a quadrangular shape, over an excavation of three or four feet in depth. The Indians along the coast, at the mouth of the Rogue followed this practice, often excavating five to seven feet, so that only a small portion of the roof was apparent above ground. The easy-digging sandy nature of the soil, and the long months of windy, rainy weather probably were responsible for their cave-like dwellings.

They lived in the same house throughout the year, not moving to summer camps as did the Takelmas. Their food was practically at their door step and there was little need for them to lead a nomadic life. Often the same family would live in one house for several generations. Those stuffy, smoke-stained dugouts had little ventilation and their dark and smelly interiors were hardly considered good examples of cleanliness and good housekeeping. Nearly all of the inhabitants were inflicted with a peculiar eye ailment. It was said that you could tell a coast Indian just by looking at his eyes. The interior tribes considered themselves superior to the "fish eaters" in every way and looked down on them with disdain.

In northern California a modified version of the same type of house construction was used by the Klamaths and

Modocs. They dug pits below the surface of the ground and roofed them over with poles. That, in turn, was covered with tules and dirt. According to some historians the circular hole-in-the-ground type of house earned for those Indians the general name of "pit Indians". Others claim their name was derived from their habit of digging numerous pitfalls in which to trap game.

Whether it was the Indian style of house construction or their method of trapping game, the early settlers in southern Oregon also applied the name to the areas most outstanding mountain landmark - calling it Mount Pit.

That majestic peak, highest in southern Oregon, was known variously by four other names: Mount McLoughlin, Snowy Butte, Big Butte and John Quincy Adams. The last was an attempt, only partly successful, to name several of the Cascade peaks in honor of our past presidents.

The inland Takelmas along the mid and upper course of the Rogue River, isolated as they were from the coast, with little, if any, contact with early explorers, were completely self dependent in their type of house construction. Until the first trappers and traders invaded their native land and they were to learn about split or hewn timbers, their houses were crude and undeveloped, though practical and servicable.

They erected a framework of vertical poles and small logs, some of which they embedded in the ground. Cedar trees grew throughout all of the Rogue region in abundance, and great slabs of the bark were easily obtainable for use as siding and roofing. It was stripped from live or fallen trees and was one of the most valuable of all materials the helpful forests furnished its primitive children. This everlasting wood was undamaged by a lifetime of abuse by the elements - and bugs and insects did not find it palatable.

The fibers of the inner part of the bark were used to weave a kind of fabric for clothing. The results were a surprisingly fine and durable "cloth" used for the most part in place of skins during the warmer part of the year.

To a lesser degree the bark of the fir was also used in house construction, as was the smooth, mahogany-colored bark of the madrona. It yielded a smooth, glossy, pliable cover in clean leather-like strips. It was water proof, and could be formed into shapes that would hold after drying - useful for many purposes.

Cottonwood, chinquapin, willow, alder - each had their use. The wood of the alder was often used for crude plates and platters as it imparted no taste or odor to food.

A hole in the center of the roof above the fire area served as a chimney. The door was simply a small opening high in the side wall. Notches were cut in poles to form steps and served as ladders to reach the elevated door. A second "ladder", inside, made it possible to reach the floor level. Pulling the outside ladder inside was equivalent to locking the door. Such door placement was also effective in keeping wild animals and marauding dogs from the living quarters and out of stored foods. The opening was covered by a skin. It was common practice to build the house so that its one door faced the nearest woods as an avenue of quick escape. Their bark and pole huts, built without floors, lashed with braided grass ropes, woven and thatched, sealed with clay and mud, were tight warm and dry.

The dirt floors of their houses surrounding the central fire area were covered with woven mats. These native rugs were generally made from a tough, springy, sharp-edged grass, that took its name from the damp, sour soil in which it liked to grow - sourgrass. Depending on the locality, it was also known as elk grass and squaw grass.

Sometimes the ceilings of the houses were also lined and sealed with mats.

Five blades of sourgrass braided together would make a tape a little over one half inch wide, or the braid might be widened to seven resulting in a width of three quarters of an inch. These braided strands when woven into floor mats, were rugged and strong - tough enough to wear for many months. The same grassy material and plaited construction was used to make basket hats that provided protection from the sun, or turned rain equally well. With reasonable care they would last for years. Cattails, or tules were used by those tribes in the lake country east of the Cascades, for the same purpose, but the supply was limited in the Rogue River Valley.

Tough and springy sourgrass also made fine material for floor pallets when topped with a skin or fur. It was the red man's mattress. Early settlers copied the Indians by stuffing straw ticks with the same grass.

The Rogues gathered a plant called vanilla leaf. Their name for it was ''Sweet-After-Death''. When mixed with sourgrass it added the refinement of giving the mattress a pleasant and fragrant aroma. This particular plant had no odor until it was picked and dried - hence its exotic name.

These were the winter houses, the ones to which the Rogues returned after the last berries had been picked, all the nuts and acorns gathered, and the fall fish runs caught, dried and smoked.

The women of the Rogue tribe were experts at weaving, braiding and skin tanning and made superior baskets of many kinds. Probably their most amazing achievement was the making of baskets in which food could actually be boiled!

"Solitude and peace-the fullness
of heart's content."

Authentic summer harvest camp.

The proper size and type of pine roots were gathered and buried in a pit, then covered on all sides with green grass and leaves. On that green covering was placed a layer of dirt and then hot rocks. A fire was built on top of this crude steam cooker. A slow, steaming, softening process would take place, eventually making it possible to string-out the fiberous root threads almost as fine as silk. Then they were braided and woven into cooking baskets. When filled with water they would quickly swell into waterproof containers.

Boiling food in the cooking baskets was accomplished by heating a supply of stones in an open fire, which were then dropped into water filled baskets with wooden tongs. As long as there was moisture in the basket it would not leak or burn.

Another source of basket material was the new growth of hazelwood. Sometimes an area of hazel growth would be purposely burned clean. The following spring, the new plants would rush to the surface and quickly grow to a height of three to five feet. This tender new growth would provide a supply of basket material that would be easy to grade into lots of similar size.

When the straight, dark-green switches were a quarter to a half inch in diameter, they were cut and peeled. This stock was used to make baskets and containers of many sizes. They were a general utility type for gathering or storing nuts, acorns, berries, or firewood. They were strong and durable and, when turned upside-down, served the double duty of stools.

Although baskets were an important item in a Rogue's home for containers, storage, and food preparation, rock bowls were used for cooking directly over a fire. The Rogues were not highly skilled at bowl making. Most of their food sources did not require grinding with bowl and pestle as did the seeds from the marsh lilies and grasses around the Klamath and Modoc lake country. Apparently the Rogues got most of their cooking bowls by trading with other tribes. The cooking bowls were nearly always in use, filled with bubbling acorn mush or stewing deer meat, kept warm for a returning hungry hunter. They were highly prized. Most families had no more than one or two. Spoons, needles, root diggers and other implements were constructed from wood, bone and horn.

The Rogues sun dried the great bulk of their foods intended to be stored for winter use, simply because it was the easiest way. Each house was equipped with a sort of storage rack suspended over the fire from the ceiling. It provided a place for meat, fish and other foods to cure by a combination of smoking and drying when the outside weather wasn't favorable. The food rack was intended only to supplement the customary outdoor drying and smoking.

At night the Rogue family sat crossed-legged on grass mats in a close circle around their fire, the men usually working on their weapons and the women weaving or braiding. As they worked, the fat from the meat on the rack would drip, drip, with regularity into their warming fire. The sputtering light would dance a pattern of shadows across their faces as they worked silently, perhaps listening to the tribe's official story teller.

Among the Rogues there were specialists in their different fields just as we have today. One of those was the tribal story teller.

He was usually an older man - one who knew every word and sign of their handed-down myths and legends. His years of experience in retelling the glories of great battles, or the mighty exploits of the tribe's favorite hunter, or the humorous antics of Coyote or Skunk, made him a welcome visitor around every campfire. He was their historian.

The achievements of each member of the village were used to an advantage. If they were outstanding, that person was dignified by being relieved of other more routine tasks. For example, someone in each village was accorded the honor of acting as official communicator between tribes.

If their physic and appearance seemed favorable, or possibly their father before them had been a runner, they were chosen at an early age. Their training started during boyhood with long hikes, often without food and water, to build stamina and endurance. As the distance increased, so did the runners ability, until it was routine to trot ten or fifteen miles without stopping for rest or drink. When the youth was ready to qualify as a full-fledged runner, he was not asked to perform any other duties around the camp except perhaps, hunt. He might, then, spend the rest of his lifetime doing little more than carrying messages back and forth from his tribe to others.

Runners were accorded the honor and privilege, at their destination, of the chief's lodge and food and usually were allowed as much rest as they wished before returning to their village.

They traveled over obscure trails known only to the red man, carrying nothing but a knife or rifle, and a pouch of buckskin containing a chunk or two of dried venison. Their ability to cover great distances was amazing, traveling continuously by night as well as day. Those wonderful specimens of physical strength and endurance could leave the Rogue Valley with a message for a Willamette Valley tribe and be at their destination in less than three days.

These couriers would, of course, be used to great advantage in time of conflict between the Indians and whites. Settlers and military men were often puzzled how the Indian could communicate so quickly with other tribes over impossible distances, much too great for signal smokes. The credit was largely due their superbly conditioned and trained runners.

Socially, the Rogues lived, for the most part, an individual life. The community structure of their villages was not highly developed, nor was it desirable. Because they lived entirely off the land, the most important thing in their lives was the continuing search for food, with skins and furs for protection and warmth, second-place.

Today, in our modern civilization we tend to live together in large communities, depending on each other to supply the goods and services we need. But with the Rogues it was different. It was a disadvantage to band together in large villages, especially during the winter months. If many families lived together in one area, it would only be a short time until all the game in the near vicinity would be exhausted. To move to another area in search of better hunting could be difficult, if not impossible, during the worst of the winter season.

So they broke-up into small groups - two or three families - searching-out a desirable location such as at the mouth of a stream where it emptied into the Rogue, or at the foot of a falls. At such places would be the best chance for winter fishing. Up and down the stream would be scattered other groups. The men might communicate back and forth several times during the course of the winter to attend council meetings, or just keep in touch with the welfare of their relatives and tribal friends.

With the coming of spring, warmer weather and easier travel, they would move out of their winter huts.

Then they would come together in one camp where they would visit and discuss the happenings of the months of isolation and prepare for the beginnings of the summer's harvest. It was the life they loved the most - moving from place to place - reaping the seasonal harvests of plentiful food and the comforts of the long, warm summer and autumn.

Beginning in the early spring many new shoots of early growth would be gathered as salad plants and eaten as greens. These "spring conditioners" would be particularly welcome after a monotonous winter diet composed mostly of dried fish and meat. Quickly following would be the spring salmon run and the early berries. Then through the summer and into the fall came the wild fruits, nuts, roots and acorns, and then another run of fish. Throughout the summer and autumn the deer, elk, bear and many smaller game animals, fat from nuts and berries, contributed their share to the Indian's diet.

The Rogues were simple in their tribal developments. There was no great amount of ceremonial practices. Each year a ritual of appreciation was held, with the first spearing of a spring-run salmon, to please the spirits and insure the continuance of future bountiful runs.

Other ceremonies, generally of a family nature, were the taking of a wife, or the coming to maturity of a girl, or a festival of preparation such as moving to a new or higher mountain camp. Even that celebration served a practical need; to feast upon any unused foodstuffs so it wouldn't have to be carried with them when they moved.

A successful hunt or fishing season was celebrated. But probably the most ambitious ceremony was that of acceptance of a new chief. Games and contests of skill were held and great amounts of food consumed. The celebrating might go on, day and night, for several days, until the food supply began to run low and the celebrants were exhausted from their efforts.

Marriage was almost entirely a matter of contract between the girl's father and her suitor. Often a purchase price was agreed upon by the parents of both, while the children were still infants. After the bride had her first child, her family presented the couple with suitable presents, but the husband had to pay an additional fee to the girl's father. It appears that financial matters presented a problem to the new husband even in those days.

It was no life of ease for the Rogue maiden. Their lot held little that was enjoyable or of pleasure. They worked every daylight hour at the many unending tasks of keeping the camp and rearing the children. They were completely dominated by their mates, had no voice in family affairs, and were required to do all the disagreeable and undesirable chores in the village. They were not generally mistreated, being regarded merely as just another item of personal property.

Their favorite activity was the freedom afforded by gathering nuts, berries, bulbs and acorns. It gave them an opportunity to go into the woods by themselves where they were unrestricted and free to visit and engage in woman talk, as much as they pleased, without the restraining influence of their men.

Many white men in a country where there were few, if any, white women, and who might have normally scoffed at the suggestion, were likely to find themselves lending support to the old gold field expression: "Say, have you noticed how much lighter them Indian girl's skin is, than when we first come to the diggin's?"

A certain percentage of Indian girls needed but little persuasion to convince them to better their living conditions by deserting their people and offering themselves to whites as willing mates. A promise of equal treatment, clothing and food, was about all that was necessary to find they were eager and anxious to get away from the Indian manner of living.

The native girls seemed to suffer no pangs of conscience or shame at being unfaithful to their kind, and often went as far in their untrustworthiness as to disclose important battle information. Western history is replete with cases in which Indian women gladly accepted the easier ways of the white man regardless of family or tribal sacrifice.

Naturally such unfaithfulness did not go completely unchallenged. To the men, however, the blow was one, more of injured pride than loss of mate. Reprisals were often not serious, sometimes not even banishment from the tribe. An interesting custom, however, was brought about as a result of Indian girls deserting their braves for white men.

With the discovery of gold in extreme northern California, that region along the mid-Klamath River proved to be one of the richest, and miners squatted on every bar and creek that had likely looking gravel or bedrock.

The Klamath River tribe had been friendly and cooperative with the whites since the first fur traders came among them, but this great new influx had brought a different type of invader.

Under the lash of the greedy whip of gold fever, big strikes and the lure of riches, the miners drove themselves through long hours of back-breaking work. At its best, gold mining is sweat and boulders, pick and shovel and aching muscles.

It wasn't long until lonely miners were offering to share their shacks and beds with Indian girls - and found ready and willing volunteers.

"Adalaid Billings –
Her spirit and memory still
live within these pages."

The chief of the mid-Klamath tribe was called Pac-kov-rhom-nic. The white miners soon reduced that long and unpronounceable name to Chief John, not to be confused, however, with Chief John of the Applegates. The chief had one daughter called Kov-rhom-nic Ef-shop-pete, and a son named Sinnah. Kov-rhom-nic was not a family name but rather the Indian custom of identifying the person with their location or village. Ef-shop-pete, roughly translated, meant "daughter of the chief". The young brave, Sinnah, long discontented with his father's peaceful attitude toward the whites, deserted his tribe and joined with the Modocs who were warriors of honor and bravery and returned two arrows for every bullet in their battles with the white invaders.

As more and more girls left their families, the chief, in an attempt to stop his tribal maidens from deserting their people, decreed that certain young girls of marriageable age must be marked with a tattoo on their face. When each girl reached the proper age, they were tattooed with three vertical stripes spaced an equal distance apart on the forepart of their chin.

This "one-eleven" mark, as it came to be called by the whites, was generally thought to be a tribal mark of identification or decoration, but its purpose was strictly intended to be one of disfiguration, with the hope of discouraging white men from being attracted to Indian girls.

The tattoos were accomplished by tapping the back of a sharp, quill-like knife of bone or horn so that its point barely penetrated the skin. Finely powdered charcoal was then rubbed into the perforated area. As it healed the tattoo turned a dark, bluish-color as if it had been painted with ink.

John Billings—
"A rare picture of the Patriarch of the deep canyon country."

Generally speaking, Chief John's method of keeping his wandering girls at home was a failure. Its effect discouraged very few whites and they continued to seek Indian girls as their mates. However, the chief didn't live long enough to realize the outcome of his efforts to curb his roving maidens.

The miners worked the easy ground first. With the richest cleaned, nearest the water, they moved back from the stream bed to the higher gravel bars.

For many years Pac-kov-rhom-nic and his band had made their main camp on a shaded and peaceful river bar which the miners were now eyeing for new operations. They asked him to move his camp, but disillusioned with the rough and overbearing miners, he refused. Lightly veiled threats had no effect on his decision. Without further parley the miners went to his camp one morning just after sun-up. Remaining out of sight in the brush, they hailed his lodge and asked him to come out. As the chief stepped through his door, unsuspectingly, into the open light, he was riddled with shot and fell mortally wounded on his own doorstep.

The miners established a renegade Indian, as chief of the camp, who was kept completely under their control with the help of an adequate amount of whiskey and a new rifle. Ef-shop-pete was about fourteen years old at the time of her father's death and due to the near breakup of the band she married, Indian custom, John Billings, a Klamath River miner.

Billings had been hearing golden stories about the fabulous Rogue River country and the rich strikes in the Jacksonville and lower Rogue area. He decided to move to the canyon country of the Rogue, sure that, because of its inaccessibility and remoteness, there would be fewer miners competing for the choice ground.

He had been reasonably successful in his mining ventures along the Klamath and was able to buy a generous amount of supplies, good mules and adaquate pack gear.

After a long, difficult trip through the mountains he and his young bride came to the Rogue Country. At the mouth of the Illinois River, near the present settlement of Agnes, he became the first white man in that area to settle on the south side of Rogue River.

There, within those rough, rugged and primeval canyon walls, Ef-shop-pete, daughter of Pac-kov-rhom-nic, lived for over sixty years, rearing a family of ten.

The source of much of the information recounted here, about the Rogues and their customs, was drawn from a vast storehouse of vivid memories this Indian princess retained and handed down through the years to her favorite grandson.

When he was a very small boy his grandmother counciled him to listen, with the "sharp ears of cunning fox", to the stories of her father's people and those with whom she had come to make their home - and how they lived in the days gone by. And he did as he was told - quite a remarkable job of it.

Chapter Three

The custom of tattooing only lightly touched the Rogues, and never the men. No face tattoos were used, but some of the older women had marks on the inner side of their left arms which were used as measures for dentalin.

Dentalin are small, peculiar shell creatures living in fragil, pencil-sized houses and are found in the sands of the northern Pacific coastal regions. They resemble tiny, curved horns or animal tusks and, in fact, were sometimes called ''tusk shells''. They are quite thin and delicate, slightly ridged, ivory colored at their pointed end, gradually darkening to sea-green at their large end. They are hollow, from one to three inches in length, and were strung in the manner of beads. Their length, coloring and condition determined their value.

Tribes along the coast of Vancouver Island were the first to introduce dentalia as a decoration. Great traders that they were, the Chinooks were quick to realize its value as trading stock and traded the shells to interior tribes, where their popularity spread east to the Rockies and into the Great Plains. At the same time, they were carried down the Oregon coast and into the interior where they were introduced to the Rogues. White traders were quick to recognize their value as a medium of exchange and carried the "shell money" as part of their trade goods, further spreading the fashion for its use.

Assuming a shell was undamaged and that its coloring was perfect, its main standard of value was its length. In trading it was therefore important that an established standard be maintained which was done by permanent measures accomplished by tattoo lines.

Another medium of exchange, limited in its use to southern Oregon and northern California, were the bright, colored feathers of woodpeckers. Not many birds in Oregon had the sharp contrast of red, white and black feathers as did those native, pileated woodpeckers. The scalp and top-knot of the saucy, red-headed noise makers were highly valued by the Rogues. They were used as a personal adornment, the scarlet color being valued to lend a distinction to headbands on which they were mounted. They provided a sharp pattern of contrast against a background of white fur. Their value was, in part, due to the fact the birds were such difficult targets as they continually circled around a tree trunk, high above the ground, scolding the hunter and at the same time keeping the tree between themselves and an Indian bird arrow.

Anthropologists tell us that the western Indian managed to exist many hundreds and in some cases thousands of years, sometimes under seemingly impossible conditions, before the white man invaded their homeland.

Most of us have at times wondered if we would be able to survive if we were magically set-down in the middle of a western wilderness without food, clothing, arms or tools. In a sense, that was the terrific handicap the original Americans had to overcome. There have been a number of instances in which such modern survival tests have been attempted, and in nearly every case they have resulted in failure.

Men reared in the west, familiar with its forests, game and plant life - aided by today's intelligence - and armed with guns and fishing tackle, have challenged the wilderness to find it was definitely no easy matter to keep alive, even in a country where natural food was plentiful.

Man's first hurdle to overcome in providing himself with food is to develop some sort of hunting weapon. Otherwise, he must adapt himself to an existence of living on plants, roots, fish and any small animals he might be able to capture. With his bare hands alone, he is a poor match competing with the speed, claws, nails and fangs of other animals.

As symbolic as the Indian himself, is his bow and arrow. Its use was standard practice over most of North America. The skill developed in the use of the bow, and various types of arrows, was determined to a large extent by the kind of game to be found in his locality. Southern Oregon, with its many wild animals, large and small, called for a great variety of arrows and arrowheads suited to a particular purpose. Because of this diversity, the Rogues were experts in the weapons they used, and particularly skillful in the art of making arrowheads.

The bows, arrows and spears of a Rogue were not just casual pieces of hunting equipment. They were his most important and valued possession and were regarded with deep respect and reverence. He humbly thanked the Great Spirit even for the wood from which his weapons were made, hoping that his piety would influence his God to speed his arrows straight and true and look with favor on his markmanship.

If a young man just starting to take his adult place in the tribe had not inherited weapons from his father or grandfather, he might spend as much as a third of his life working to complete a full set of hunting and war weapons.

We moderns, whose products are children of mass production and precision machinery, find it hard to even imagine the painstaking work and uncountable hours it took to shape even one perfect arrow shaft. It becomes a bit easier to understand the Indian's feelings for his weapons when it is realized that a single arrow shaft with an imperceptable amount of flaw, might veer from its flight enough to result in a missed target and possible death from a charging wounded animal or a hostile warrior. Handicapped as they were by the crudeness of their tools, and the time involved, there was still no substitute for perfection.

The finest shafts were made from native white oak. Its slow and torturous growth furnished a wood, when properly heat-treated and seasoned, that was as near to metal in strength and toughness as it was possible for wood to be.

The process of manufacture was a personification of patience. First the oak piece - straight and clean - free of knots and imperfections, and large enough that when the shaft was finished it would be wholly from heartwood. Then came the tedious process of curing, tempering and shaping. After the shaft had been carefully scraped until all the sapwood had been removed, heating and scraping accomplished both shaping and seasoning. Slowly and carefully, just the right amount of heat was applied and the process continued, over and over again, taking off only a fraction at a time. A perfectly straight, perfectly round arrow might take weeks to complete - but what a pride to own! Doesn't the phrase "straight as an arrow" now take on a new meaning?

The toughness and flexibility of oak would allow it to bend without breaking and return to its original trueness. It could usually be removed from its victim without risk of damage to the shaft. A hunter or warrior would always retrieve his prize arrows if at all possible.

Spruce and hemlock were often used for arrows of less importance - small game - such as squirrels, rabbits and birds. These woods were not as hard as oak and less time, effort and perfection would be used in their manufacture.

Everything that has been said about the meticulous care used in shaping arrow shafts was transcended by the precise and exacting art of making arrowheads. Here, indeed, is a lost art. It is one that should be classed with today's skill of fine gem cutting and jewelry making. It is doubtful, if in Oregon today, there are many people who could give a detailed description of chipping an arrowhead. It is also quite likely that few if any, could actually accomplish the feat using the Indian's methods and means.

The stone most commonly used was a hard, brittle volcanic rock from the quartz family known as jasper, often mistakenly called flint. Its dull, opaque color ranges through various shades of brown, red, yellow and white - sometimes even variegated. This native stone, which actually has a hardness exceeding steel, was not too plentiful in the Rogue Country. Small deposits were found in the Josephine Creek area, while more liberal amounts were scattered from higher lava flows in northeastern Jackson County.

The Rogues fashioned most of their arrowheads and spear points from this flint-like rock, although its texture was such that, even with care, many were broken in manufacture resulting in misshapen arrowheads. Usually such pieces could still be used to arm less important arrows even though the barbs might not be perfectly matched. Many were refashioned into smaller points, without barbs, for use as bird arrows.

Greatly superior to the Oregon jasper for all kinds of weapons - knives, spears, ax heads and scraping tools, as well as arrowheads - was the highly prized jet-black obsidian. A volcanic product resembling glass more than rock, it was often referred to as "glass rock".

This glassy off-spring of molten lava flows could hardly have been more suited to fine arrowhead making if specifications had been set forth in detail and in some special way manufactured for that sole purpose.

The paramount advantage in making arrowheads from obsidian was the fact that it would always chip with a conchoidal fracture. In non-technical language that means when a chip is broken off it will be shell-shaped, leaving a concave reverse pattern on the original piece. Due to this unique characteristic of always chipping with the same kind of fracture, a definite quality control in rock shaping was possible, not found in other types of jasper or quartz.

About fifty miles east of Bend are two rock mountains known as ''Glass Buttes'' which were the primary supply of obsidian for much of Oregon. This celebrated obsidian producing region has been recognized as the most extensive in the world, not only in the basic black type, but in many other colors of gem-like quality - translucent in larger pieces and nearly transparent in thin sections. There is evidence that these deposits have been worked extensively and used as a manufacturing and distribution point for many thousands of years.

The Rogues traded with the Shastas, who in turn perhaps dealt with the Modocs or Paiutes or other tribes living along the fringe of the Oregon desert country. Rogue traders might travel as much as two or three hundred miles carrying prize furs, skins and other trading stock, bringing back all of the treasured black quartz they could carry. Such long trading journeys were not uncommon, at least before the coming of the white man.

The one indispensable tool used in making arrowheads was the deer-horn hammer. The pointed end of a deer horn was cut off and a wood handle attached with thongs, making a tool somewhat similar to a prospector's pickaroon. The point of the horn hammer was then beat with just the proper force squarely against the smooth surface of a rock. The end of the horn gradually shattered, replacing the solid end with sharp, needle-like slivers not unlike our modern nylon bristles. It slowly assumed the form of a tapered point. These fiberous steel-like splinters were extremely tough and durable. They were only a fraction of an inch long.

As a Rogue warrior prepared to make an arrowhead, he first tended his fire of hardwood until its heat was as even as if his fuel had been coal. Then carefully he heated his rock to just the right temperature. His thermometer was hours and days and years of experience. Next he dipped his heated material in tepid water - not too cold - once again just the right temperature. Many tiny invisible fractures spread web-like in the surface of the rock, the amount of heat and the temperature of the water determining the depth.

Now began the actual chipping. With the point of his horn hammer he carefully pecked at a small area. Little flakes, thin and sharp, would fly off as the horn fibers pried into the minute cracks like tiny wedges. These shell-shaped flakes, resembling fish scales in size and thickness, were like bits of shattered glass. The rough shaping continued until the depth of the heated fracture had been reached. The piece was then returned to the fire and reheated.

As the heating and chipping continued certain portions of the rock were chipped away, while others were allowed to remain. A slow shaping began to take place with the arrow's point and barbs emerging as more material was removed.

As the piece began to resemble the finished product greater and greater care and patience was necessary. Too much heat, water too cold, or blows too hard might shatter the structure too deeply and many hours - even days - of previous work lost as the head broke apart.

Long before the final chipping began, the piece was no longer completely dipped in water or heated on all sides. More intricate shaping now required that the water be applied only to the exact spot where material needed to be removed.

As the area became smaller and the work more precise, the tip of a feather was used to apply a fraction of a drop of water to the exact spot where only one or two chips might need be removed. Those chips could be removed so precisely and with a pattern so identical, that the sloping edge along either side of the arrowhead could be finished with tiny, evenly spaced teeth like a fine saw blade! When one remembers that a perfectly shaped game or war arrowhead had three points, not one, two of them being rear barbs, some idea of the tremendous amount of skill, patience and time required can be realized.

Another beautiful example of the excellence of workmanship and the care and persistence it must have taken to make them, were the delicate points for bird arrows. Some of them long, slim and perfectly formed like ebony teardrops, were shaped with the precision and beauty of a cut and polished gem. There are beautiful examples that are no more than one half inch long and barely a quarter of an inch wide!

The method just described was used when the finest of prize hunting or war arrows were made. It is quite possible to chip and shape certain types of quartz and obsidian using only the sharpness of a nail point or hardened horn or bone. By prying and pushing against the material, small flakes may be removed much the same as if it were glass.

Although fine weapons for hunting and war and the skill to use them were a related part of every Rogue brave, they still did not depend entirely on their arms to supply all their needs for meat. Much of the taking of big game was done with pitfalls - some with snares. Concealed and camouflaged spears, set up along trails on which animals would impale themselves, while fleeing in fright before a drive, was quite effective in taking elk and deer.

Although spears were an important part of every Rogue's arms, they were considered a secondary war weapon to the bow and arrow. That was not true of the fishing spear, however, for its use was of great value in taking salmon from the creeks and streams. It was an interesting and quite highly developed instrument and the Rogues were expert in its use. The fishing spear was never thrown, always hand held.

The most important part of the salmon spear was its point. A few inches of the sharp end of a deer horn, with its slight, natural curve, would be cut off on an angle. That provided a hollow socket in the horn which was enlarged, rounded and fitted closely, but not too tightly, over the end of a spear shaft. The pointed end of the horn was sharpened. A buckskin thong was fastened around the center of the horn in a circular notch and to the lower part of the shaft.

Waiting at the lower edge of a falls, in the shallow waters of a spawning riffle, or on a projecting rock or ledge, the Rogue fisherman developed amazing accuracy in spearing salmon. Their range was deadly for any fish swimming within six to eight feet from them. They learned to compensate with absolute perfection, for the image distortion of parallax, when gauging the underwater depth and distance of a swimming salmon.

When the spear was driven through the fish, its wild flopping or a quick jerk on the spear would cause the horn point to pull from the shaft. The fisherman then had his catch on a short length of thong, with the spear point acting as a toggle or barb. The fish would be unable to pull the barb through its body and the spear gave leverage in landing the catch with the flexible thong acting as a short length of fish line.

Most of the salmon catch was taken in this manner with little, if any, time spent on trout. Fishing provided one of the necessities of life and was not considered a pastime. Sport fishing had not as yet come into its own as recreation and entertainment.

Salmon, for the most part, was sun dried. Sometimes it was boiled or smoked, but not usually cooked or mixed with other foods. Huge amounts were cured for winter use by splitting the fish down the back and belly to the tail. They were then cleaned and filleted, turned "inside out" and hung across poles to dry. As unpalatable as it may seem to us, it was also common to eat salmon raw.

The Rogue River, in its abundance, furnished still another product - the long, slimy and repulsive looking eels that appeared in the river with the early salmon run. These snake-like fish were extremely rich in oil and their fat was used as a seasoning. Eel oil, in a cup-shaped rock, soaked into a wick, would also provide a crude, smokey, smelly light.

Eels were easy to catch by hand on shallow spawning riffles, or by diving into deeper water and pulling them from rocks where they would attach themselves by their ugly, flat sucker-shaped mouths. Their flesh, though edible and prized by some tribes, was little used by the Rogues as food, probably because of the abundance of salmon.

A delicacy in the shellfish kingdom was the crawfish. Searching for them under flat rocks, in shallow water, ready to scurry backward at the first sign of danger - plowing up a screen of mud as they tried to escape - provided hours of hunting and entertainment for little Indian boys. After being tossed into boiling water the shells were cracked away from the claws and tails, disclosing a pink, sweet, delicious meat very similar to saltwater shrimp.

It would be natural to assume that venison and other wild game, together with fish, would be the Rogue's first and most important supply of staple food. But as important as they were, it may be surprising to learn that acorns comprised the primary ingredient for several forms of meat, soup and mush diets. The great advantage of the acorn stemmed from the fact that, when properly cured and prepared the red man had a food product usable in several ways and capable of being stored for long periods of time.

The most desirable acorns came from the Sadler oak, sometimes known as the sweet oak. This scrubby, low growth oak, normally under eight feet in height, was found throughout the Siskiyou and Coast ranges. It was usually a dependable and heavy producer of nuts and its acorns were mild in their content of bitter, tannic acid, compared to the more widespread black oak. The nuts could be combed directly from the shrubs or gathered from the ground as they fell. When they dropped in a natural manner they were immediately gathered, for if they weathered on the ground for a short time, the bitterness was less objectionable and the deer, bear, squirrels and other animals found them to their liking.

The canyon, live oak, was another type, a little more difficult to gather, but also low in tannic acid content. The tanbark oak, was still another low-growing source of acorns. Every available basket, container, and storage area was filled to overflowing during the fall harvest season.

Most of us when children, recognized the acorn as a nut, but having tasted them found their bitter, puckery, taste was conductive to a fair amount of spitting and sputtering. The Indians, their taste little different from ours, knew how to overcome this difficulty.

After the caps had been removed from the acorns special large wicker baskets, with spacings just less than an acorn in size, were filled with nuts. They were then sunk in a river or creek bed where moving water would continually wash through the loaded containers. This steady filtering and blanching process would leach-off and wash away most of the undesirable acid taste, making the nuts edible. Then they were shelled and thoroughly dried and then pounded and ground into a course meal. From that meal, several nourishing and palatable dishes were made.

Always a common food in every lodge was acorn mush, or soup, depending on its consistency, and ingredients. Often venison was added and the product became a meat stew. An even more popular and improved version was made by pounding and grinding dried venison into a meal and mixing it with the acorn porridge. To that, might be added some dried and ground madrona berries, to lend a degree of sweetness to the taste. Sometimes wild onions were included for a flavor variety, or one of several kinds of mint.

After boiling the acorn meal and meat mixture with its seasonings until it was quite thick, it was shaped into cakes and baked before a fire on hot rocks. When the cakes were brown and completely dried, they could be stored for months, serving as a valuable and nourishing part of their diet during the winter months, when game and fish might not be plentiful or easy to take.

Pioneer arctic explorers, long ago realized the value of this native pemmican. By using wheat flour and adding ground raisins to the various other ingredients, it provided an easily stored, easily carried food, on which they depended heavily, during long periods of isolation without fresh food and vegetables.

With the Rogues, as with many other Oregon tribes, the camas was their most important vegetable. That native substitute for potatoes was particularly nourishing and delicious when prepared in the proper manner. It grew throughout extensive portions of the west and was partial to open, moist, meadow lands. It was once a common sight to see Oregon fields covered with the lilac-blue camas blooms during the month of April.

The edible part was actually a bulb, resembling an onion in shape, and from one half to two inches in diameter. The camas bulb was dug in the late summer and fall by the women of the tribe, locating the plant by the dried seed top and popping them out of the ground with a sharp-pointed "camas stick" which had previously been hardened and tempered with fire.

They were prepared by pinching off the tops and wrapping them in several folds of green, maple leaves. A package of, perhaps, a half-gallon of bulbs would be prepared at a time. A hole was dug in the ground and lined with more green leaves. Hot rocks were placed at the bottom. Packages of the leaf-wrapped bulbs were put in this native oven and covered with more leaves and dirt. A fire was built on top of the oven and kept going for two or three days. When the pit was opened a delicious aroma would arise from the dark brown camas. The taste of the potato-like bulb is similar to yams, perhaps even sweeter, and is sometimes compared to white figs.

If the baked camas was then boiled slowly for a long time, the thick resulting syrup would be sweet and molasses-like. It was often kept for festive occasions and used as a treat for the children, in the same manner we might use candy.

The early settlers were familiar with the taste of camas and often relieved the monotony of their diet with a covered dish of bulbs, similar to a sweet potato pie.

The Rogues were a fortunate tribe to live in such a bountiful country. In no other part of the Oregon Territory was game more plentiful or varied. There were several varieties of deer. The great monarch of all horned animals the noble elk, were numerous, as were antelope, mountain sheep and goats. Black bear, cinnamon bear and the most formidable of all, the great grizzly freely roamed the hills and valleys of the Rogue Country.

Where there was much game there was always cougar and wild cat and wolves. Hoards of smaller animals were found in every locality - coyotes, gray foxes, raccoons, badgers, porcupine, rabbits and squirrels. For furs, the Rogues depended on the beaver, otter, martin and mink. For still more variety there were ducks, grouse, quail, pigeons and doves.

The Rogues never hoarded food, secure in the feeling that natural supplies would always be adequate and available. Then too, they moved often and had little or no means of transporting large amounts of stored provisions.

Huckleberries and blueberries were found in large amounts and were dried for winter use - other varieties were eaten fresh. They seldom cooked or dried any food that could be eaten raw, except those intended for winter storage. The dried berries were often eaten without stewing or softening with water.

The wild strawberry, sweet as honey, the huge juicy, thimbleberries, the heady aroma of the seedy blackcaps and that unforgetable flavor-nectar of the midget, low-vining blackberry, were all there for the picking.

There were meaty blue-black serviceberries, with their big black seeds, the delicious salal berry, and the rambling wild grape, straining its way to the very tops of reaching oaks and maples to drink golden sunshine to trade for purple sweetness.

Huckleberries, with their odd, wild aroma, were abundant in several varieties - thumb-tip size and dark blue in the Cascades, to a smaller and lighter colored variety along the coast range. There was also an early red type - juicy and tender - compared to its darker cousins. Blueberries were found on their low-slung vines in generous amounts in the higher altitudes west of the Rogue Basin, and were particular favorites for drying.

Madrona and manzanita berries each had their purpose. A novel and interesting use was made of the hard, tart-tasting reddish-green manzanita berry.

Unlike other berries it does not drop from the bush as it dries, but clings until all that remains is a thin dried shell, filled with a powdery, cream-colored dust mixed with a few seeds. These dried berries were picked and crushed in a small basket-container. That, in turn, was placed inside a second water-tight basket, and filled with water. The floury manzanita mixture was allowed to dissolve and soak through the water. It was then used as a refreshing cold drink. The taste had a sharp, tanginess something similar to ginger ale. It was not intended to be used medically; only as a pleasant drink as we might use lemonade.

Wild nuts were a great favorite and many were gathered. The hazelnut grew in abundance and was the most popular. Gathering them was woman's work. The squaws would make annual trips to coastal region hazelnut camps, where they would stay two or three weeks. The nuts were dried in the shell after beating off the outside hull with flails. The chinquapin was a close relative of the hazelnut, but not as numerous.

The prize delicacy of all were the sugar pine nuts. Small and difficult to gather, they were the caviar of the nut family. If the cones bearing those delicate morsels were allowed to open normally while on the tree, the seeds would flutter to the ground on a membranous wing, supplied by mother nature so the wind could scatter them more effectively.

Most squirrels love pine nuts and work every daylight minute storing them in their winter larders. Blue jays, flickers, grouse and pigeons also offered more competition for the rare little tidbits.

Just before the cones were mature enough to open they were knocked to the ground by any method that would succeed; climbing trees and dislodging them with long poles; shooting them down with bow and arrows; or waiting for an obliging squirrel to cut them down, and then retrieve them before the squirrel could. Sometimes they would find a squirrel's cache and rob it of its stored treasures.

Newly picked cones were still green, very pitchy and difficult to handle. They were held over a fire until the pitch was burned away. That was also just enough heat to cause the cone to open its folds. If it was then tapped with a stick and shaken vigorously the seeds would fall out. Everyone liked pine nuts, young and old alike. They were greatly enjoyed around the warming fires during the long winter nights.

The Rogues ate no lizards, snakes, snails or rodents; mother nature kindly setting a more attractive and generous table. There was one delicacy, however, that was both exotic and interesting and would likely cause today's eyebrows to arch. Grasshoppers!

They were gathered early in the season when the insects were adult, but had not developed wings. The first step in preparing them for eating was to pull off their head and hopper-like legs. This was done in one operation. When the head came off, all the insides fastened to it also came out.

After cleaning they were put into a tight basket and hung high over the fire. They were very rich with a fatty oil. The slow, steady heat caused the oil to come to the surface, actually cooking them in their own fat.

They were said to be quite delicious, having a taste like a nut - a rich, oily nut. Unless their parents watched them closely, it was quite common for the children to over eat on the rich insects, making themselves sick.

If a Rogue did get sick he was far from helpless in treating himself. His doctor and corner drug store, was once again, that great provider - mother nature. For most of the common ailments he had some kind of cure or treatment.

That Indian boy with the upset stomach might be made to drink a tea brewed from the princess pine or blackberry root. Oregon grape was boiled to make a tea for dysentery. It was also used as a tonic. Chittum bark was chewed just as it came from the tree, without first being dried. The plant with the Spanish name, yerba buena, or good herb, was used extensively even by the pioneers. It was such a popular cure-all it became known as ''Oregon Tea''. Chewing pine gum was a sure cure for worms; and cascara bark was used by those braves with a tired run-down feeling.

If none of these cures worked there was always the sweat house as a last resort. This peculiar custom was more than just a health treatment. It was the approved method of driving evil spirits from the body which caused the sickness. However it was not considered a religious ritual to be practiced on any regular or special occasion. It might be possible for an Indian to go through all his normal life and never feel the need for a sweat cure. Its practice and effectiveness was never questioned, probably because the patient either recovered or died. And what can be more positive than that?

The house was usually a small affair, built out of anything that was handy - skins, mud, poles and bark. The walls were tightly sealed with mud and clay to contain the steam. It was constructed near the banks of a river or stream where water was handy. A fire was built on the outside of the house and many large rocks heated. These hot rocks were carried inside and plunged into baskets of water, until the house would be dripping with moist heat and steam.

Although the squaws tended the fires and kept the steam bath going they were not allowed the use of the steam room. It was a closed club - a privilege accorded strictly to the men. Most villages had at least one sweat house - some, two or three.

The naked Indian would parboil in the moist heat until sweat would be pouring from his entire body. Then he would emerge on the run and jump into the stream. As most of their sickness occurred in the winter the water would be icy cold. If he lived through the shock, it was positive proof that all the evil and destructive devils had been driven out of his body, and that he would recover. One thing was certain - if he was hardy enough to survive, then he MUST have been cured. If the treatment value is questioned, one fact is positive; it was at least, a great "leveler" removing the unhealthy from the camp. It was responsible, at least to some extent, for the fact that there were seldom many old men other than chiefs, seen in Indian camps - but many old women!

TIRZAH TRASK

Chapter Four

The customs and beliefs concerning life, death, Gods, devils and sickness, were dictated almost entirely by the witch doctors in most western tribes. But that custom seems to have been little practiced by the Rogues. The chief of the tribe, or sub-chief of the band, decided such issues when they pertained to the treatment of ailments or the spiritual well-being of their people.

Their religious and spiritual beliefs were simple. They did not engage in extensive rituals or ceremonies. They constructed no totems, nor did they leave any carvings or idols of worship. Yet some of their beliefs were surprisingly parallel to that of the white man.

They believed there was one supreme being - a Great Spirit - to whom each of them were accountable if they were to reach their place in heaven. They believed in many destructive devils, there being one responsible for nearly every phase of trouble or hardship a Rogue might encounter. It was their custom to believe that the spirit dwelling within the body of every Rogue would leave that body on the third day after death.

Someone, usually members of the family or a close friend, would sit with the remains of the deceased, never at any time leaving the body alone, until three days had passed. During this mourning period many hours of unearthly, wailing incantations were performed. Sometime during the third day, a shadow - or spirit - ascended from the body. After that the body had no more earthly value and could be buried.

Seeing the spiritual shadow leave the body was a very positive thing to a Rogue - never imagined. The image might even be different from the body's present form, sometimes it being that of a child, signifying only a different time phase in the person's life.

The dead brave was dressed in his best skins and surrounded with his most personal and favorite ornaments such as beads and jewelry. He was furnished an adequate amount of food, so that his spirit would be well provided for until it reached the land of promise. Arrowheads, a knife - perhaps a stone ax - have been found in graves, but no instances of a full set of weapons; they were too precious and valuable.

His heaven was a place of abundance, furnishing all his wants and needs and an everlasting life. It was a true "happy hunting grounds" although that term was one applied to the Indian's heaven only by the whites.

Even as with the white man's religion, a Rogue did not automatically go to his reward. In his past life his conduct must have been such that, he was considered a "good Indian". The requirements were simple but positive.

Bravery and honesty were the highest attributes. To be a brave and noble warrior when called upon to defend and protect his family and tribe was of great importance. But such rules were not binding in his dealings with his enemies. The same was true of stealing. To be caught stealing from another tribe was permitted - even encouraged and treated as a sport. But to steal from his own tribesman was a dishonor, unforgivable, and could result in banishment. Honor also demanded that he be a good hunter and provider for his family and for other tribe members in need. These few simple beliefs, were all that was required to insure him a place in the hereafter.

Burial was always underground and the grave well rounded with dirt and rocks. No burials in trees or above ground were ever practiced. If ground burial was not possible, as in the case of battle, the body was cremated.

No Rogue ever took his life by suicide, for that was sure to incur the displeasure of the Great Spirit. There was, however, a form of mercy death that was sometimes carried out.

If for example, a Rogue had grown too old and infirm to keep up with his tribe during their moves, he might request that he be left in a camp or in the shelter of a cave or windfall, with a small supply of food and water. The decision whether the act would be permitted, was not decided by him or his family, but by the tribe council. Severe? No, it was the law of the primitive. And it was recognized that survival and strength were words of the same meaning.

If it was necessary to determine how serious an occurrence of tribal infraction might be, it was the responsibility of the chief and his sub-leaders to make that decision. A meeting of the tribal heads was held every twenty-eight days, marked by a certain moon phase. All the problems concerning the tribe that had arisen since the last meeting were discussed at the council. After the decisions had been made, the meeting was thrown open to all tribe members and the results were made known. Such decisions were final - there were no appeals - but that did not mean that they could not be tempered with mercy. After the business of the council was completed the meeting ended in general festivities and feasting which might continue for the rest of the night.

Despite the war-like and treacherous reputation applied to the Rogues by early trappers and settlers, there is much evidence to indicate that before the coming of the white man, they lived in peace and contentment in their beloved Rogueland.

In general, they got along well with their neighbors to the south, the Shastas and Klamaths, and with the Umpquas to the north who were generally a peaceful and friendly tribe. The coast tribes carefully stayed on their side of the mountains, as did those east of the Cascades.

Actually, there were no known acts of torture or cruelty that was a part of the Rogues conduct toward the people of their own tribe or others. The one universal practice of unexplainable cruelty, attributed to so many Indian tribes - scalping - seems to have not been a practice carried out by the Rogues prior to the invasion of the white man. There is reason to believe that it was an adopted custom, introduced by early white scouts, or their Indian counterparts, from tribes eastward of the Rockies.

Slavery among Indians was common. It was practiced in varying degrees by many Oregon tribes but the word "slavery" does not properly describe the methods used by the Rogues in these activities.

It is true they sometimes conducted raids on other tribes, carrying off desirable, strong young girls. But that was a normal procedure, intended to strengthen tribal blood lines and was practiced to some extent by all tribes.

During these raids they might also capture a brave who had earned a reputation as an expert canoe maker, or one highly skilled in some phase of weapon making, or any of many accomplishments that could strengthen and benefit the tribe in general.

The prisoner would be securely guarded on his return to the Rogue's camp but in no way mistreated. In fact, that was the key to the whole operation - to induce the captive to become a satisfied member of the Rogue family. Restraint on his freedom was quickly relaxed, and extra privileges of special food, choice furs and skins and the most desirable mates were offered to convince him that his lot was better with the Rogues than with his own people.

If their efforts failed, he was allowed to "escape" and little was lost. But more often than not, the newly-drafted brave would find himself satisfied and happy with his new life and added prestige with his adopted friends.

If such means to an end seem alien to the general beliefs of Indian practices, one must remember that slaves, if forced to perform menial and degrading tasks of a type usually only expected of women, needed to be continually guarded, lest they escape.

The men of the tribe had no time to waste guarding slaves. For if they must do so, who would do the hunting, and fishing and make the arrows and repair the spears and bring in the food? These were unending daily chores, always a part of their existence and it was necessary that their performance be carried out with routine regularity.

These, then, were the people, and their customs, and their way of life - those that dwelt in the land of the Rogue. They were as much a part of that natural wilderness of primitive beauty as were the other wild creatures that roamed the forest homes that roofed the sky above them.

Great sheltering forests they were, the softness of their pine-scented breath as soothing as the quiet murmur of their gentle streams, kitten-toeing across soft beds of unhurried moss.

And circling all around that land of secret green valleys and flower trimmed meadows, rose a great wall of protection, erected there just for the Rogues.

Later, when the invader forced his way into that last deep corner of Oregon sunset, they cursed that wall in anger, and called it mountains, and the creatures who dwelt there in freedom and contentment, they called savage and wild.

Do you think, perhaps, the Rogue Valley might have been created at sundown, on the sixth day?

ARTIST CREDIT

The author is indebted to Chester Adamson of Laramie, Wyoming, for his expressive and factual drawings for the cover and chapter headings of this book.

PHOTOGRAPH CREDITS

Chief "Tyee" John	courtesy	Siskiyou County Museum
Tirzah Trask	courtesy	Oregon Historical Society
Teepee by river	courtesy	Oregon Historical Society
Adaline Billings	courtesy	Leo Frye
John Billings	courtesy	Leo Frye
The River Scenes	courtesy	E. Morgan Abel

ACKNOWLEDGEMENTS

The author wishes to gratefully acknowledge the historical contributions and help of the following persons and publications.

Howard Bearss	Grants Pass
Russel Bigelow	Grants Pass
Mildred Bryce	Grants Pass
Elwin Frye	Cave Junction
Al Greenwood	Grants Pass
Robert Mansfield	Grants Pass
Frank Woolridge	Grants Pass
Leo Frye	Powers
U.S. Bureau of American Indians, North of Mexico	F.W. Hodge
Handbook of American Indian Languages	F.W. Hodge
Tribal Sketches of Southern Oregon Indians	George M. Cochran
History of the State of Oregon	H.K. Hines D.D.
History of Oregon	Charles H. Carey
Grants Pass Daily Courier	Grants Pass
Gill's Dictionary of the Chinook Jargon	J.K. Gill Co.

Other Unforgettable Books By Percy Booth:

THE LEGEND OF INDIAN MARY AND UMPQUA JOE

by Percy T. Booth / ISBN 1-885813-01-5 / $7.95

This 60-page volume is the story of Indian Mary, a Rogue Indian who lived in the deep canyons of the Rogue River and operated a ferry at the present site of Indian Mary Park. The book also contains pioneer pictures of the area and other historical stories of early trailblazers.

UNTIL THE LAST ARROW

by Percy T. Booth / 1-885813-06-6 / $ 19.95

This is a 500-page historical novel of the rough and tumble days in the Rogue Valley, the first true complete chronicle of the early 1800's and the bloody Indian wars of Southern Oregon. The volume is lavishly illustrated with more than 60 pioneer photographs and a map of the Rogue Valley in the early days. Large 6x9 format.

GRANTS PASS, THE GOLDEN YEARS

by Percy T. Booth / ISBN 1-885813-02-3 / $9.95

Hardbound / ISBN 1-885813-05-8 / $19.95

A pictorial study of the City of Grants Pass from its early days. Many of the photographs were printed from the Booth collection of glass negatives.

ALASKA DIARY

by Percy T. Booth / ISBN 1-885813-08-2 / $9.50

It was 1944. War raged in the Pacific. In Unalakleet, Alaska, author Percy Booth and his wife Ruth worked in harm's way at a lonely wind-whipped outpost radio station on the Bering Sea. The 78-page diary style volume tells that story including powerful black and white photographs taken by the author.